A
NEW
RESONANCE

5

Edited by
Jim Kacian & Dee Evetts

A New Resonance 5
Emerging Voices in English-Language Haiku

Red Moon Press © 2007
ISBN 978-1-893959-65-1

Red Moon Press
P.O. Box 2461
Winchester VA
22504-1661 USA
www.redmoonpress.com

Cover Painting: Jose-Augusto França Millares
Painting, 1956
Mixed Media, 81 x 100 cm.
Private Collected, Madrid.
Used with permission.

Foreword

When we began this project we thought it was a one-time event. Here now into our fifth volume, featuring eighty-five poets over ten years, we are aware of the fine community we have had the pleasure of coming to know at the beginnings of their careers. Far from imagining its ending, we are pleased to recognize that this is only the start of connecting with these new voices in the haiku world. In fact, to celebrate this special group, we have created a new companion volume to *A New Resonance* entitled *echoes* which is intended to keep the group in contact with one another as well as to carry its legacy from one generation to the next. It is select company, and we know we will look back at this series one day and recognize the quantity of talent which was first exposed in these pages. Nothing could give us more pleasure.

Jim Kacian & Dee Evetts
Series Editors

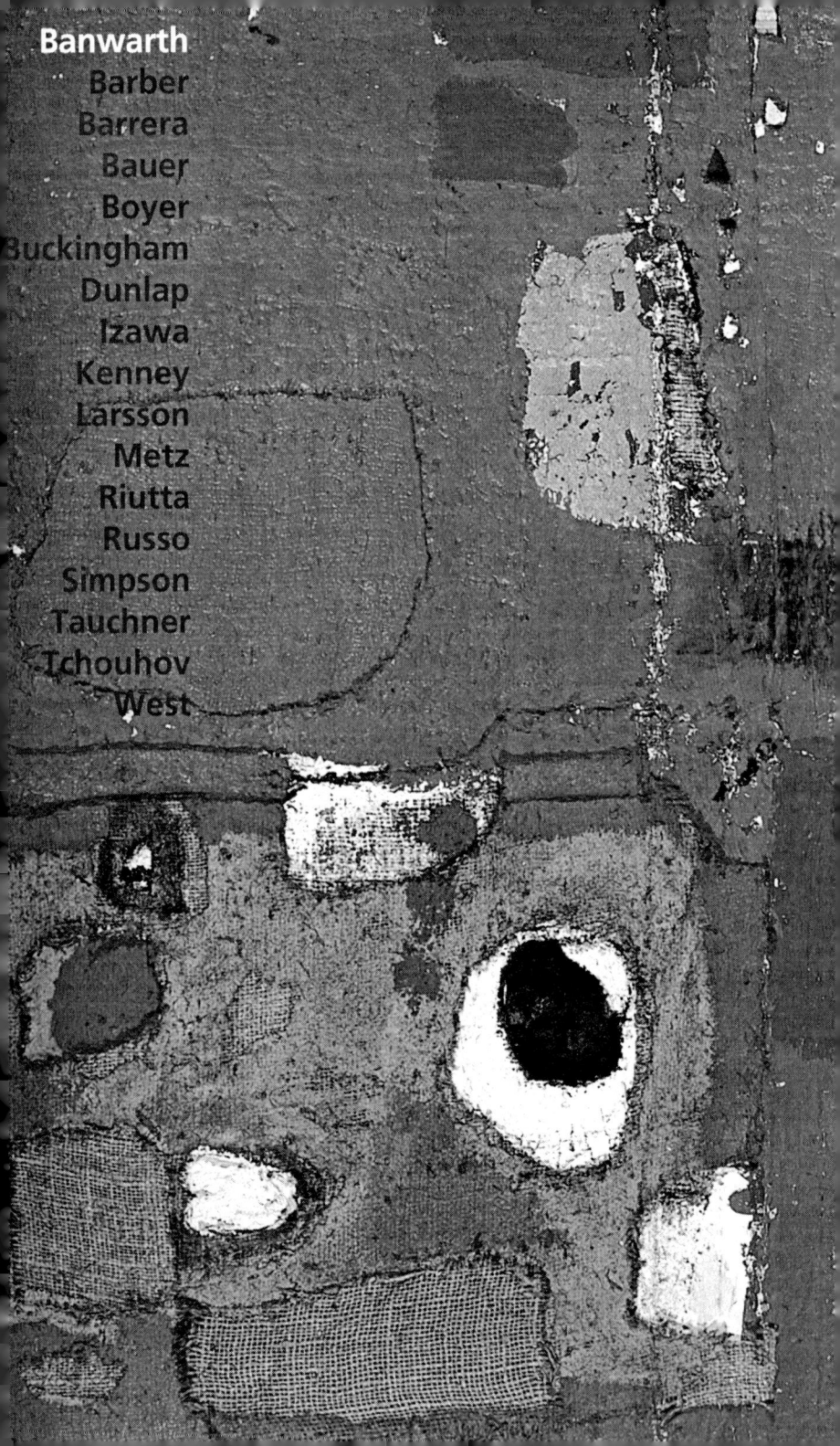

Francine Banwarth

Proofreader/Copy Editor

Born 29 June 1947
Los Angeles, California
Currently resides
Dubuque, Iowa

Banwarth is not new to haiku, as many New Resonance poets are, but returns to the genre after a long hiatus. She has had remarkable success in recent contests, and paradoxically this might be an impediment to discovering her strongest work, since poems that win contests do not automatically best convey one's voice. The work found here bespeaks a yearning, and a reaching for that which eludes. But this is not a source of frustration for the poet so much as an inspiration to move beyond complacency toward that enigmatic future at which we are all pointed.

Credits

cloudy day	Drevniok Haiku Contest 2001
brushing	*Midwest Haiku Anthology*
dogwood in bloom	Frost Haiku Contest 2005
a flock of birds	*Frogpond* XIX:2
summer moon	Weiss Haiku Contest 2005
a circle of light	*Brussels Sprout* VII:1
August twilight	*Modern Haiku* 36:2
we let	*Modern Haiku* 38:1
slipping them in	HSA Members' Anthology 2004
peep holes	*Asahi Evening News* Jan 2000
Pleiades at dawn	Tokutami Haiku Contest 2005
child's wake	Henderson Haiku Contest 2005
first night of snow	Drevniok Haiku Contest 2001
at the piano	HEA Senryu Contest 1992
confession	Kaji Aso Haiku Contest 1992

"summer moon," "dogwood in bloom" and "child's wake" each took first place in their respective contests; "at the piano" took a second; "Pleiades at dawn" and "first night of snow" thirds, and both "cloudy day" and "confession" honorable mentions; "a circle of light" was an Editor's Choice for its issue.

cloudy day
giving the prism
a twirl

brushing,
her small hands gather
the weight of my hair

dogwood in bloom
our daughters running
out of their shoes

a flock of birds
among the raspberries
she couldn't reach

summer moon
cellist holding the breath
of the bow

a circle of light
the long necks of swans
        dipping in

August twilight
he reminds me
of my shortcomings

we let
    the wine breathe
        slow moving clouds

slipping them in
before the autumn moon
. . . onions

peep holes
in the kiwi vine
neighbor comes and goes

Pleiades at dawn . . .
talking each other to sleep
near the river's edge

child's wake
the weight
of rain

first night of snow
sifting through
his box of old buttons

at the piano
my son practicing
the same mistake

confession:
she knots
his tie

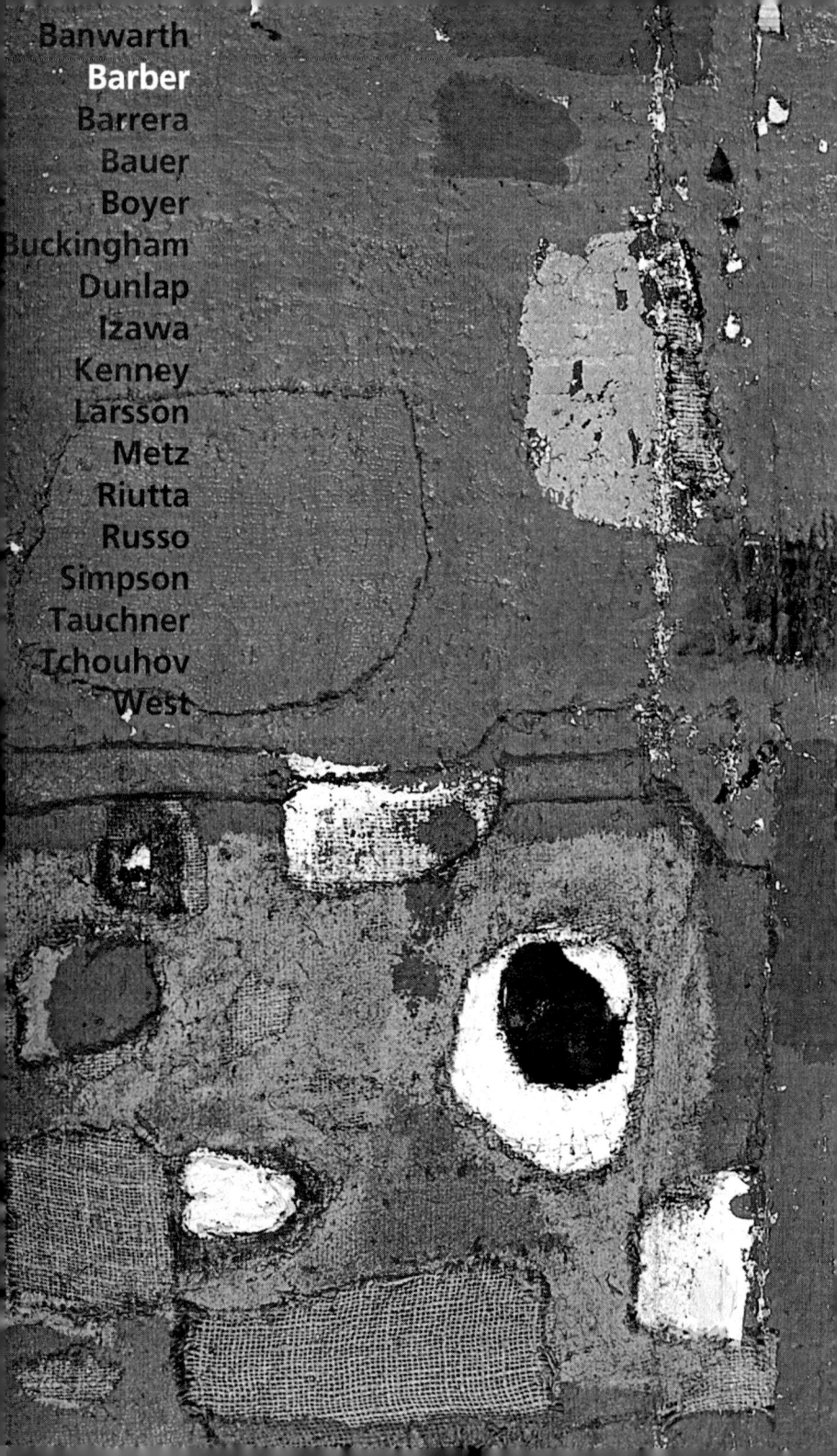

Collin Barber

MRI Technologist

Born 13 November 1974
Memphis, Tennessee
Currently resides
Marion, Arkansas

It is apparent that Barber is new to haiku—anyone who could coin the phrase "haiku money" must be—but his poems read as though they come from an old hand. His particular strength is to transform our expectations with an ironic twist, often in the most mundane of circumstances. He exhibits a keen sense of consequence for actions taken, or not taken. We may also detect a rueful willingness to play the fall guy, thus revealing himself to be a canny poet of relationship.

Credits

honeymoon	*Frogpond* XXX:1
summer clouds	*The Heron's Nest* VIII:3
spring fever	*Chrysanthemum* 1
a shopping cart	unpublished
one more game	*The Heron's Nest* VIII:2
a cloud briefly takes	*bottle rockets* 16
one color left	*Shiki Kukai* August 2006
city skyline	*contemporary haibun online* 2:4
Indian summer	*Modern Haiku* 37:3
morning chill	*Modern Haiku* 38:3
autumn morning	*Frogpond* XXIX:3
the ant returns	*The Heron's Nest* IX:2
snow flurries	unpublished
mistletoe	*Chrysanthemum* 1
another first date	*Shiki Kukai* September 2006

"city skyline" also appeared in *contemporary haibun Volume 8;* "Indian summer" also appeared in *big sky: The Red Moon Anthology 2006.*

honeymoon over my suntan peels

summer clouds
she talks about death
hypothetically

spring fever the thermometer's long red line

a shopping cart
in the handicap space—
hard summer rain

one more game
of shirts vs. skins
summer dusk

a cloud briefly takes
  the shine from the bleachers
    seventh inning stretch

one color left
in the Popsicle box
summer's end

city skyline a shooting star's dead end

Indian summer
a bottle cap replaces
the missing pawn

morning chill—
I move to her side
of the argument

autumn morning
I still have the tooth
I lost in my dream

the ant returns
after being flicked . . .
autumn loneliness

snow flurries
my haiku money
in the vending machine

mistletoe—
the familiar lip
of a cold bottle

another first date . . .
I fail again
to be myself

Janelle Barrera

Teacher

Born Unlisted
Wadley, Alabama
Currently resides
Key West, Florida

Barrera's work here hinges on two basic conerns, the sense of belonging in or to any given place, and the difference that sharing one's geography with another can make. She is a keen-eyed and unsentimental observer, and her persona shows sufficient self-confidence and feistiness that we suspect she will never settle, but continue to search for the best of both matters. Even then, these satisfactions will not prevent her from continuing to ask, where on earth would I like to be? And with whom?

(Photo by Marina Hightower)

Credits

the hottest day	*Solares Hill*
fiery red these flame trees	*Solares Hill*
trying on toe rings	*Hermitage* 3
ebb tide	*The Heron's Nest* VI:8
walking off regret	*Modern Haiku* 35:3
boarding the Greyhound	*The Heron's Nest* VII:3
ocean-front room	*Hermitage* II
between me	*Frogpond* XXVII:2
floating on my lawn	*Solares Hill*
autumn woods	*Modern Haiku* 37:2
evening rain	*The Heron's Nest* VII:4
winter drizzle	unpublished
rain-streaked windows	*Modern Haiku* 35:3
at the poetry guild	*Frogpond* XXVIII:2
lingering winter	*Frogpond* XXIX:2

"evening rain" also appeared in *inside the mirror: The Red Moon Anthology 2005*, "at the poetry guild" also appeared in *big sky: The Red Moon Anthology 2006*.

the hottest day
she brings me mangoes
and stays and stays

fiery red these flame trees
and the island sun—
staying for the summer

trying on toe rings . . .
the street vendor says
they're me alright

ebb tide . . .
the other tracks in the sand
also mine

walking off regret . . .
an hour or more since
the sun and sea darkened

boarding the Greyhound . . .
one seat left
on the ocean side

ocean-front room—
we argue a bit over where
the sun will rise

pink winter sun . . .
new to the island
she feeds the gulls

floating on my lawn:
the neighbor's mahogany
leaf by leaf

autumn woods—
at my sister's house
I wear one of her sweaters

evening rain
the new phone book
without his name

winter drizzle . . .
sending his Christmas card
to his mother's address

rain-streaked windows . . .
a round-trip ticket
as cheap as one-way

at the poetry guild
they ask if haiku
is all I have

lingering winter . . .
renewing my subscriptions
to everything

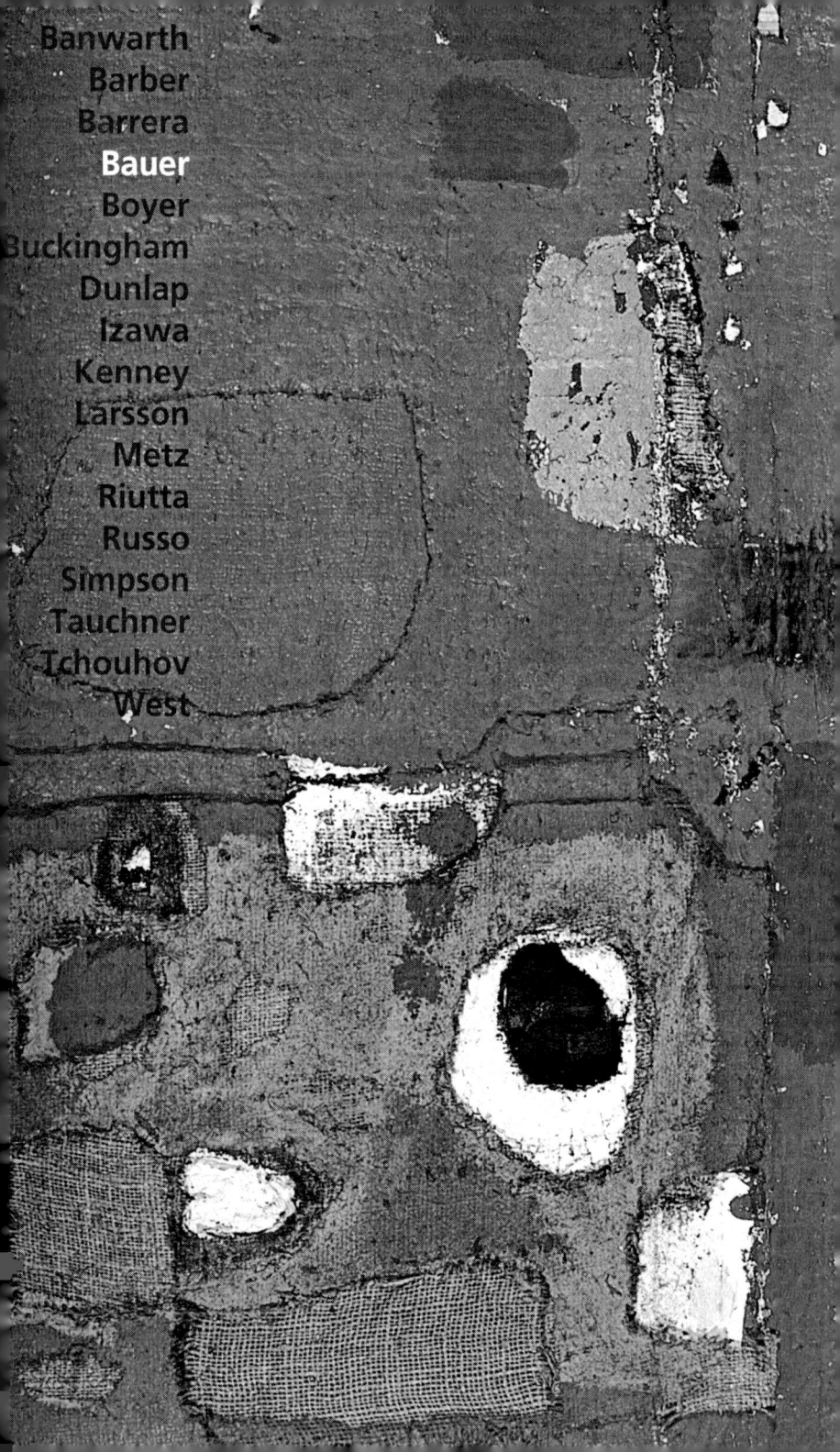

Robert Bauer

Carpenter/Electrician

Born 4 July 1953
Pittsburgh, Pennsylvania
Currently resides
Big Wheeling Creek, West Virginia

Though haiku is considered the poetry of nature, the writers of haiku have become increasingly urban and removed from the natural world they extol. Not so with this poet, whose work is steeped in the relative wilderness of West Virginia. Bauer notes the little collisions between creatures and their environment, and delights in the revelations they afford, showing a particular affinity for animals, including the human animal, at work and play. His occupation takes him into the elements and grants him the opportunity to make these observations at first hand.

(Photo by Debra Bauer)

Credits

first snow	unpublished
gust front	unpublished
light snow	unpublished
noon whistle	unpublished
the long day	*The Heron's Nest* VI:9
winter sunset	unpublished
cold moon	unpublished
rutting season	unpublished
tooth marks	*The Heron's Nest* VII:1
Lenten Moon	*Shinzounokodou* 2
lingering snow	unpublished
grease oozes	*The Heron's Nest* VIII:3
midsummer	unpublished
a mud wasp crawls	unpublished
autumn sunrise	*The Heron's Nest* VII:4

first snow
the gypsy slips some beans
into her mojo

gust front
the lineman strips a wire
with his teeth

light snow
I add slaked lime
to the mortar

noon whistle
a cardinal swerves
through the laser

the long day—
a mason drizzles mortar
between flagstones

winter sunset
a rusted wedge
stuck in oak

cold moon
coyote pups slide
across the creek

rutting season—
a streak of cinnamon
in the applesauce

tooth marks
in the sharp cheddar . . .
the long night

Lenten Moon
wilted ivy curls
on a satellite dish

lingering snow
my wife paints daisies
on a butterfly house

grease oozes
from a Ferris wheel
the long day

midsummer—
the uneven whirl
of a hula hoop

a mud wasp crawls
out of the wind chime—
summer's end

autumn sunrise
the scent of sage lingers
in the prayer lodge

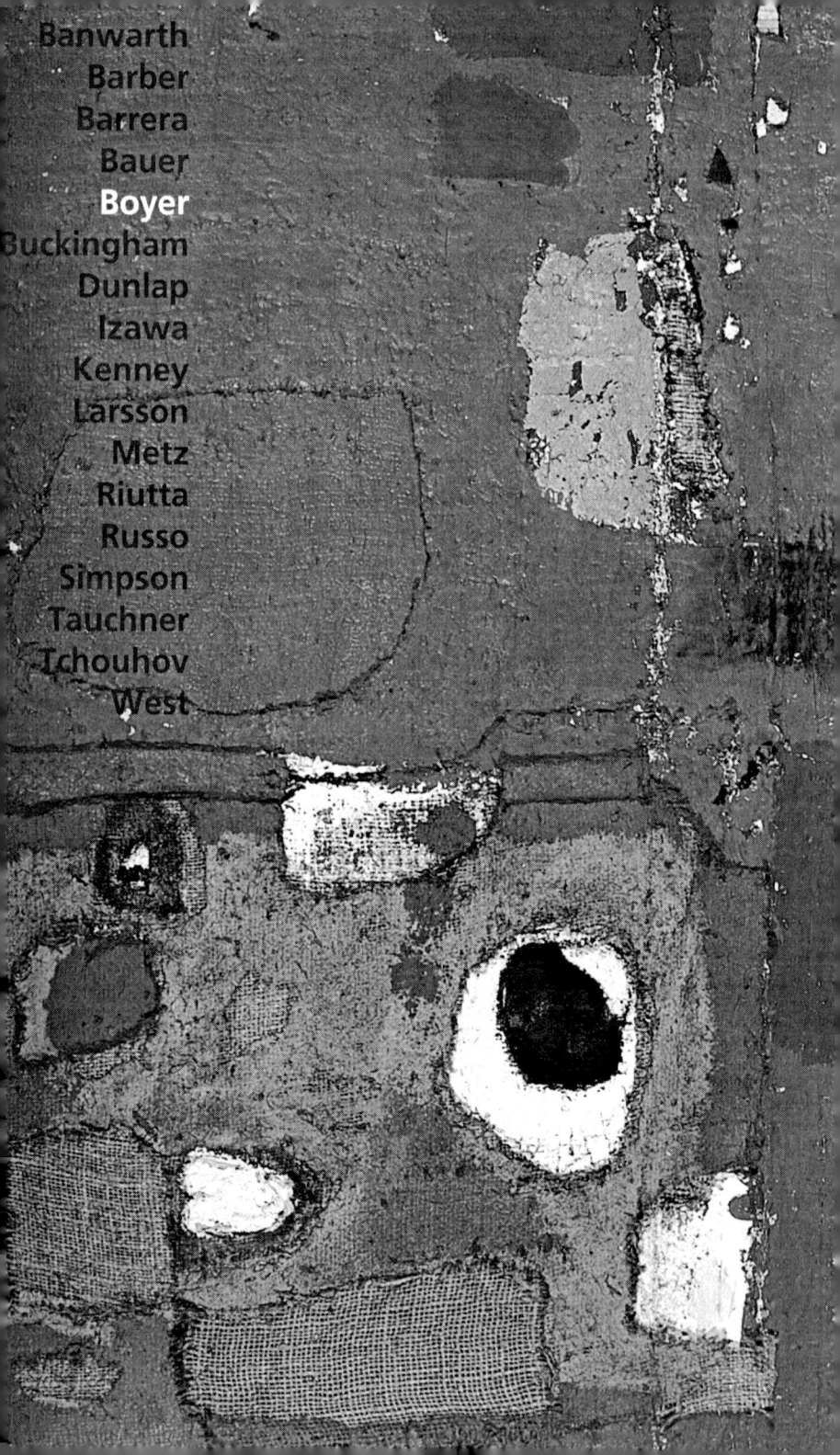

David Boyer
Research Editor

Born 17 January 1974
Pottsville, Pennsylvania
Currently resides
Stamford, Connecticut

Boyer's work is a testament to faith, the kind of hopefulness in the face of ambiguity that is most essentially human. Like all of us, he is confronted by the imponderables of life—relationship, meaning, aging—and even when his own chosen symbols seem to argue against it, he finds the means to hesitate before acting rashly, to anticipate before giving up. And this outlook, perhaps even despite himself, can't help but take on an optimistic cast.

Credits

crickets in the breeze	*Acorn* 16
haze burns off	*bottle rockets* 15
her hand on my chest	*Frogpond* XXIX:2
the teabag squeezed	*Acorn* 18
carefully lifting	unpublished
workmen slide	unpublished
a gnat	*Frogpond* XXIX:3
her sarcasm	unpublished
still August night	*Modern Haiku* 37:1
crickets	*Paper Wasp* 12:1
the dishwasher	*Paper Wasp* 12:1
the town's broken clock	*Modern Haiku* 37:1
church bells	unpublished
the moon	*Paper Wasp* 12:1
half a speckled egg	*bottle rockets* 14

crickets in the breeze
I decide to wait
another day

haze burns off—
meaning to answer
that letter

her hand on my chest
in the laundry room—
the short night

the teabag squeezed
till bursting—
another year older

carefully lifting
the new glass bowl—
my hands on your hips

workmen slide
shingles to the ground
twilight lingers

a gnat
floats in tequila
night heat

her sarcasm
lost
in the stars

still August night
staring into the light
from the fridge

crickets
in the cool breeze—
sleeping alone

the dishwasher
halfway through
a dream of the ocean

the town's broken clock the color of the snowstorm

            church bells
            far away in black
            the year turns

                        the moon
                        and one dim star—
                        counting my change

half a speckled egg
in long grass—
the walk home alone

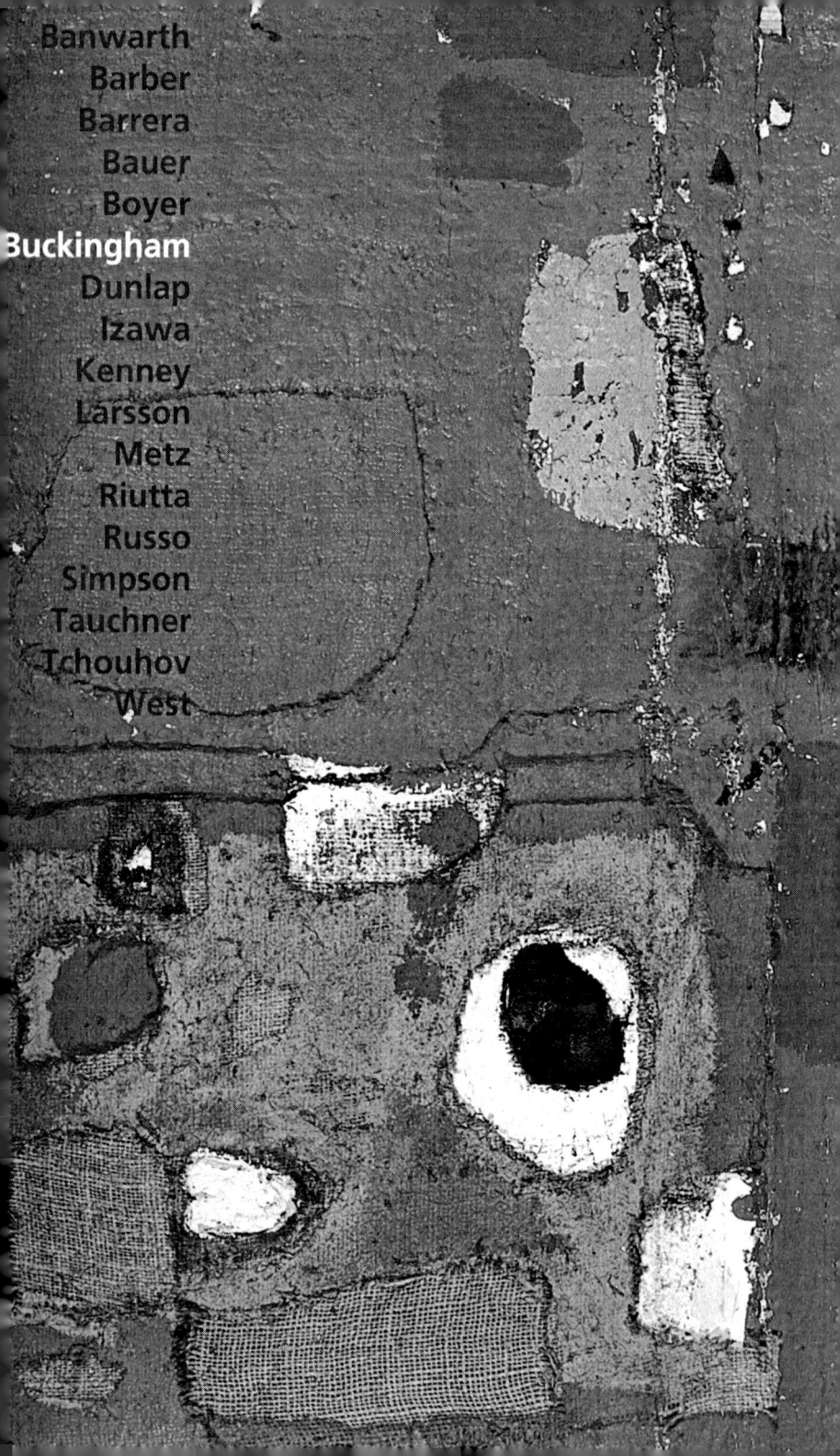

Banwarth
Barber
Barrera
Bauer
Boyer
Buckingham
Dunlap
Izawa
Kenney
Larsson
Metz
Riutta
Russo
Simpson
Tauchner
Tchouhov
West

Helen Buckingham

Writer

Born 17 February 1960
London, England
Currently resides
Bristol, England

Haiku has been called the poetry of what is, and if we are able to hold to it truly, it can help us see just where we are. To be able to articulate something is to begin to own it. Buckingham's work achieves a balance that helps her meet the challenges we all face, and adds the wide vistas that can overcome a merely parochial sense of existence. The poet perceives a half-full cup, which is, of course, a chosen position, one which haiku accomodates.

(Photo by Richard Kevern)

Credits

Leonids night	*Roadrunner* VII:1
Christmas at the Mall	*The Heron's Nest* VII:4
Chinese New Year	*The Heron's Nest* VI:10
summer vacation	*Lynx* XXI:1
dozing	*Modern Haiku* 35:2
summer's end	*Acorn* 15
old school	*Roadrunner* VI:4
back outside	HIA Haiku Contest 2003
graffiti	*The Heron's Nest* VII:1
results morning	*Snapshots* 12
tracing the contours	*Frogpond* XXVII:2
Indian summer	*Roadrunner* VI:4
first night	*Snapshots* 12
breakfast shift	*Acorn* 12
Visiting Day	*Modern Haiku* 37:2

"back outside" won Honorable Mention in the 5th HIA Awards in 2003; "Indian summer" also appeared in *big sky: The Red Moon Anthology 2006*; "breakfast shift" also appeared in the *Snapshots Haiku Calendar* 2005.

Leonids night . . .
picking a pomegranate
clean

Christmas at the Mall . . .
the turkey steps forward
with a clipboard

Chinese New Year—
daring to call my sister
   a monkey

summer vacation—
paintwork
dripping paint

dozing
by the radio . . .
another Hottest Day

summer's end . . .
jazz on board
the ferry

old school
the coldness
of the triangle

back outside
the gallery . . .
an endless sky

graffiti
sharper
by moonlight

results morning:
the mulberry tree
a deeper green

tracing the contours
of my brain scan . . .
recalling past mountains

Indian summer
another half-cup
left in the flask

first night . . .
the life model
still in her robe

breakfast shift
. . . sharing the last
of the stars

Visiting Day—
her diary
   left open

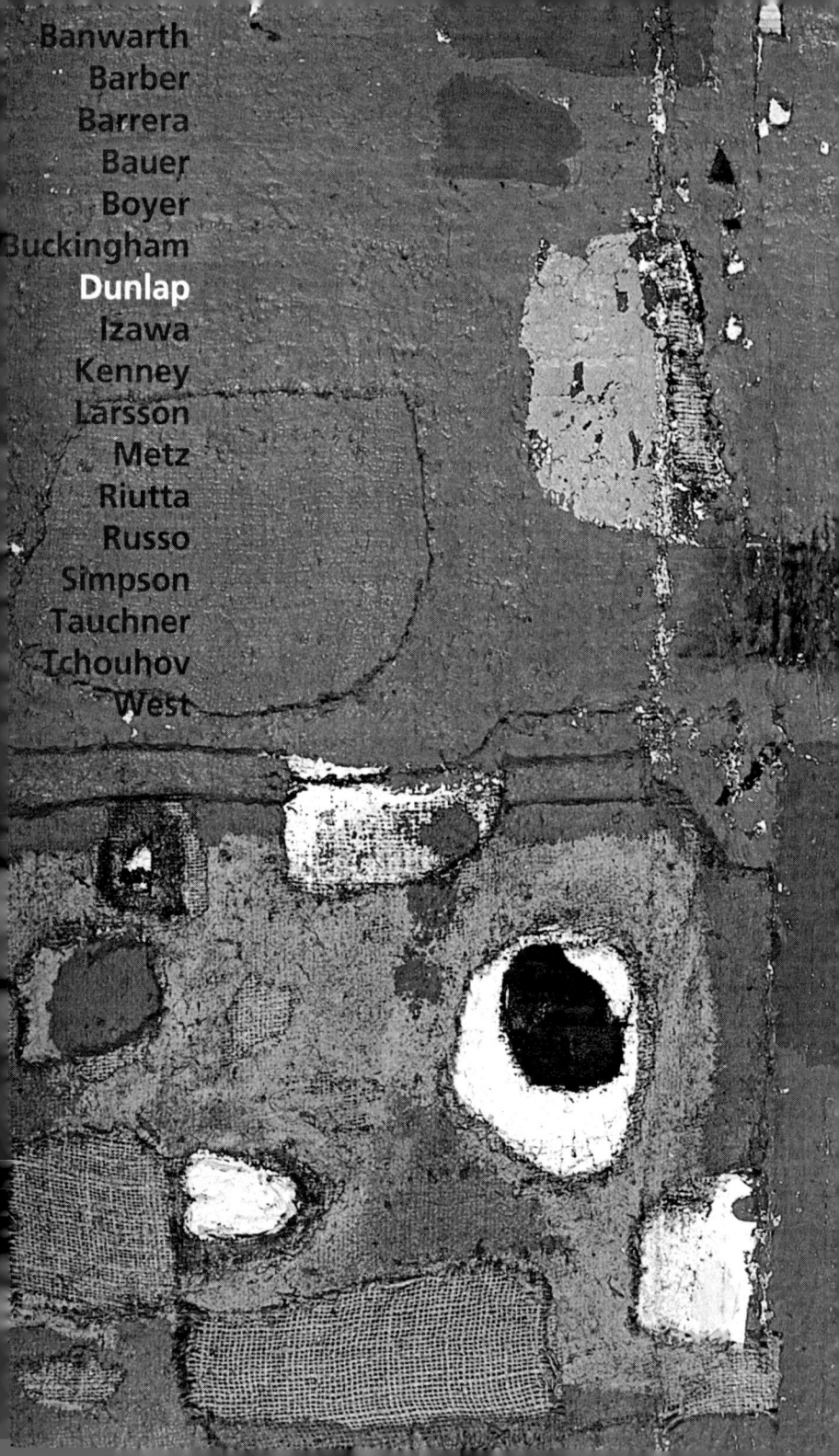

Banwarth
Barber
Barrera
Bauer
Boyer
Buckingham
Dunlap
Izawa
Kenney
Larsson
Metz
Riutta
Russo
Simpson
Tauchner
Tchouhov
West

Curtis Dunlap

Systems Administrator

Born 3 November 1957
Reidsville, North Carolina
Currently resides
Mayodan, North Carolina

A sense of personal history can be a great motivator—toward a fulfilling goal, away from an unworthy past, or perhaps continuing a favorable status quo. Dunlap is a poet whose past is fully at his disposal, and he is keenly aware of choices made, and the effects these choices have had. He is aware, too, that his decisions will carry only so far, that try as he may he will not always keep up. While there is the occasional bliss of a vacation from these hard truths, the better measure is what he hands on, not the least of which will be these poems.

(Photo by Dave Russo)

Credits

ocean sunrise	*The Heron's Nest* VI:6
fog rising	*The Heron's Nest* VI:11
scent of diesel	*Frogpond* XXVII:1
weathered footbridge	*Modern Haiku* 38:1
late summer drizzle	*The Heron's Nest* IV:11
vacation's end	*The Heron's Nest* V:10
secluded highway	*Modern Haiku* 35:1
forked lightning	*Valley Voices* 6
a gray cubicle	*The Heron's Nest* VI:9
family reunion	*The Heron's Nest* V:4
after the burial	*The Heron's Nest* VIII:4
autumn chill	*Frogpond* XXVI:3
cycling with my son	*The Heron's Nest* VII:4
insomnia	*Frogpond* XXVII:2
a new school year	*The Heron's Nest* VI:10

"after the burial" also appeared in *big sky: The Red Moon Anthology 2006;* "cycling with my son" was an Editor's Choice for its issue.

ocean sunrise—
we flip shells
with our toes

fog rising—
mushrooms push aside
a bed of pine needles

scent of diesel—
the tugboat's wake
rolls into shore

weathered footbridge—
a penny glimmers
in the current

late summer drizzle—
evening walkers
slow their pace

vacation's end—
windshield wipers in synch
with the radio

secluded highway—
in and out of my headlights
a John 3:16 sign

forked lightning—
a black snake slithers
into the bird house

a gray cubicle—
cicada songs
through a speaker phone

family reunion—
wild turkeys
among the headstones

after the burial . . .
my father's smile
on so many faces

autumn chill
the crack of an acorn cup
under a shoe

cycling with my son—
this is the autumn
I fall behind

insomnia—
a receding train whistle
lengthens the night

a new school year—
one long blast
of the bus driver's horn

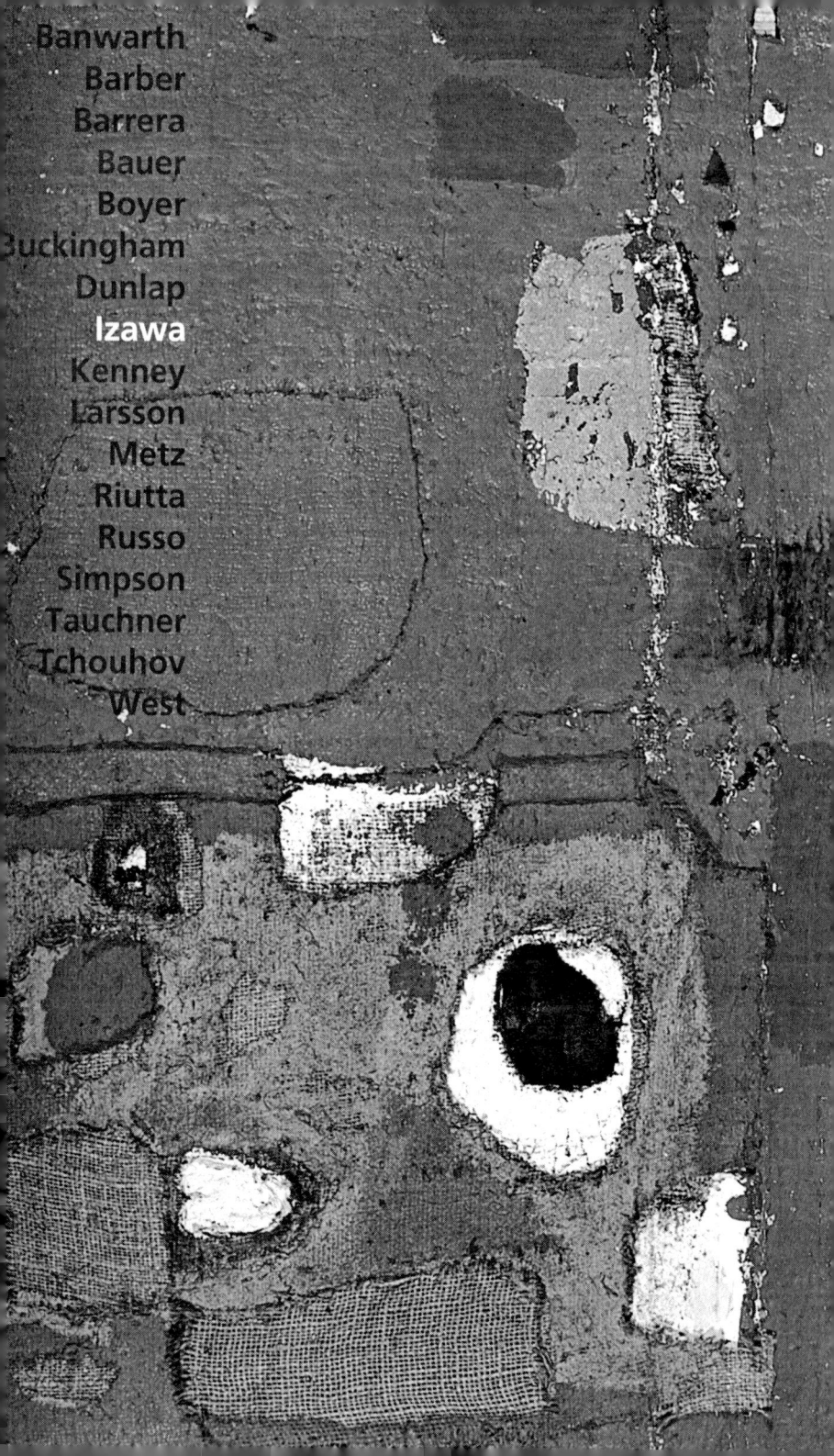

Keiko Izawa

Technical Translator

Born 16 November 1952
Yokohama, Japan
Currently resides
Yokohama, Japan

Japan is in the throes of a cultural revolution, effected largely along generational lines. Those in the middle generation, insistent upon neither the old values nor the new, have a difficult line to walk, belonging to neither. The poet is a barometer to this change. How, when poised between conflicting sets of values, does one risk the whole weight, be faithful to the whole person? These are the issues in Izawa's work, and all the while we can hear the clock ticking for her, faintly.

Credits

flipping	*Clouds Peak* 2
high school reunion	*The Heron's Nest* IX:3
morning dew	*Haiku Harvest* Fall 2005
lost in thought	*Simply Haiku* Winter 2005
ice skating	*Simply Haiku* Winter 2005
cold night	*Presence* 30
spring sunlight	*Presence* 29
balmy spring day	unpublished
summer fireworks	*Haiku Harvest* Spring 2006
gathering dusk	unpublished
red moon	*Simply Haiku* Winter 2006
pounding rain	unpublished
evening	*Clouds Peak* 2
island night	*Presence* 30
south wind	*Presence* 29

flipping the remaining pages
of the calendar
september wind

high school reunion
we view the falling leaves
in different ways

morning dew . . .
in the autumn wind
a newborn's cry

lost in thought . . .
in the empty sky
kites cross

ice skating
into his hand
my whole weight

cold night
I quietly loosen
the guitar's strings

spring sunlight . . .
in the baby's toy box
a long-lost key

balmy spring day
two young wives discuss
a bamboo-shoot recipe

summer fireworks
the night of the unfolding
peony

gathering dusk . . .
in the abandoned boat
an unfinished bottle

red moon . . .
reciting to myself
the samurai's death poem

pounding rain—
realizing I'm on
the wrong train

evening . . .
the ambulance siren
lingers in town

island night . . .
writing alone
coughing alone

south wind
a postcard from my friend
with her new name

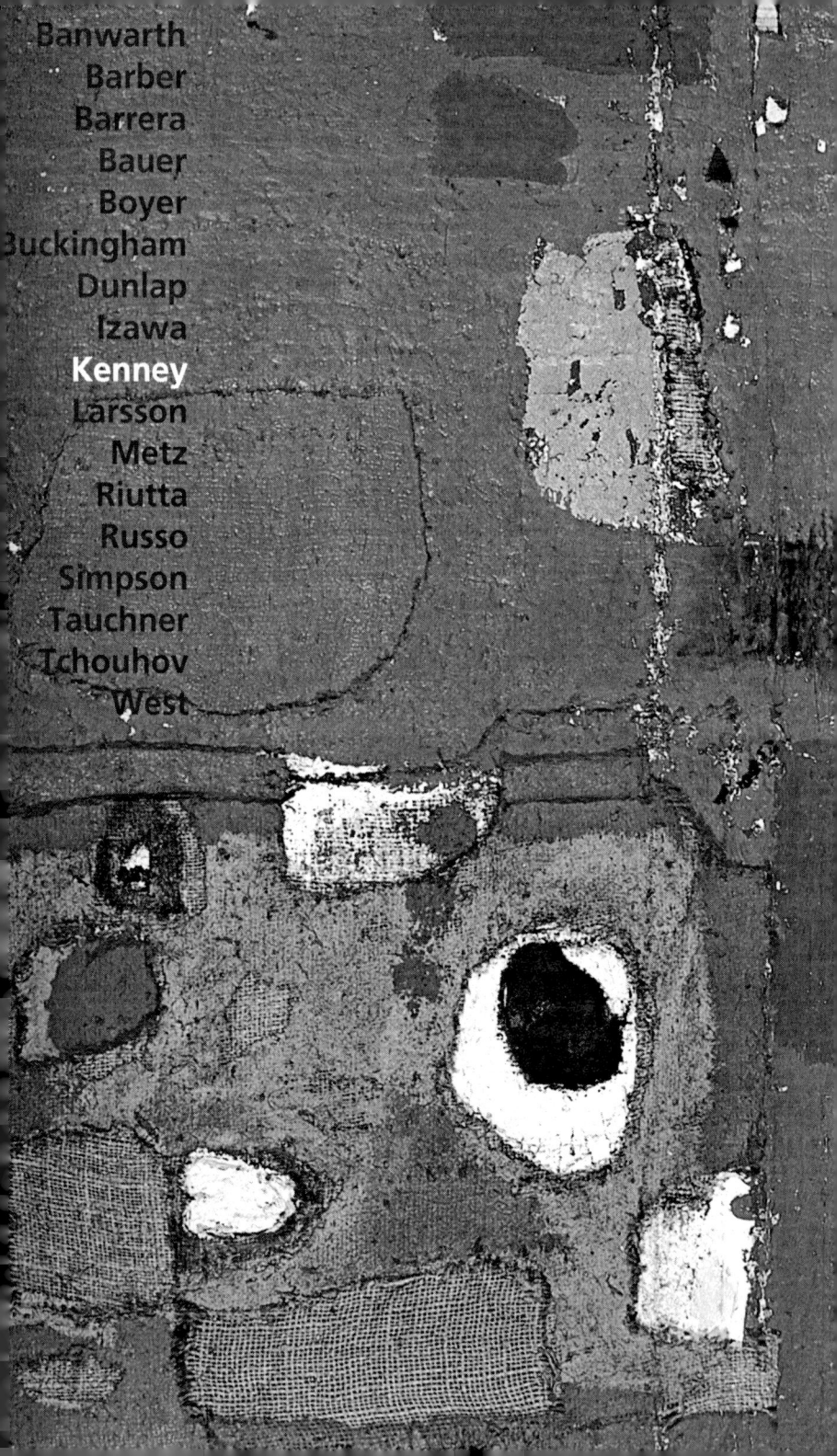

Bill Kenney

Academic (Retired)

Born 29 January 1933
Newton, Massachusetts
Currently resides
Queens, New York

Often when a poet is at home in his environment it will not be the obvious visual changes in his landscape that he marks, but the inconspicuous—things unseen but deeply felt. In Kenney's work this focus emphasizes the interchange between the sources of meaning, the ephemeral and the cyclical, the occasional and the eternal. He has a particularly keen awareness of these tensions, and how they affect family and faith. He cannot help but ask, over and again, what it is that can be kept, and what must be let go.

(Photo by Patricia Kenney)

Credits

kite in the wind	unpublished
old photograph	*World Haiku Review* 2007
sky writing	unpublished
silence	unpublished
mosaic	unpublished
summer dusk	unpublished
home for a visit	*temps libre* 1 January 2007
abandoned factory	unpublished
sunset	unpublished
winter surf	unpublished
new year's party	*temps libre* 1 January 2007
first snowflakes	unpublished
Epiphany	unpublished
a friend's ashes	*temps libre* 1 January 2007
spring morning	*Shiki Kukai* March 2006

"spring morning" also appeared in *big sky: The Red Moon Anthology* 2006.

kite in the wind
that moment of wanting
to let go

old photograph
my wife's face
before she knew mine

sky writing
a word taken
by the wind

silence . . .
each waits for the other
to start the quarrel

mosaic
in a darkened church
my prayer

summer dusk
children at play
calling "May I?"

home for a visit
the sound of rain
on the river

abandoned factory
parking spaces
marked "Reserved"

sunset
the pay phone
stops ringing

winter surf
the ocean
takes it back

new year's party
the divorced couple
leaves together

first snowflakes
turning to catch
your smile

Epiphany
the neighborhood returns
to ordinary darkness

a friend's ashes
heavier than I expected
winter wind

spring morning
the thrust of roots
through a sidewalk

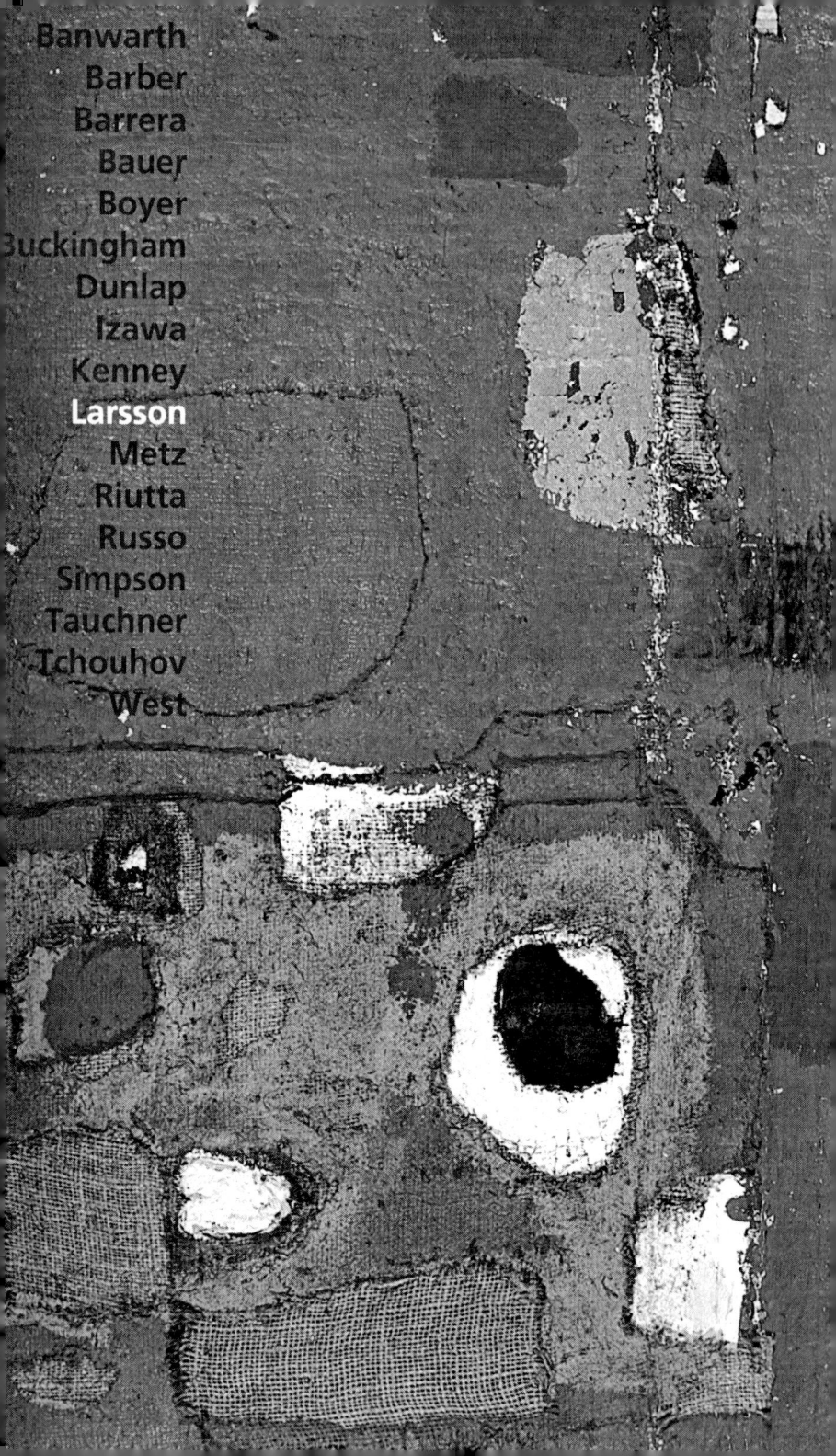

Marcus Larsson

Design Manager

Born 23 July 1961
Ljungby, Sweden
Currently resides
Vaxjo, Sweden

Larsson's gifts of eye and ear are evident in these poems, but it is empathy that is his most telling attribute. He balances a sensitivity toward relationship with a seasonal aspect that feels completely unforced. The result is a poetry of natural affect imbued with emotion and in a unique voice, quietly but tellingly getting to the heart of the matter.

Credits

spring morning	*The Heron's Nest* VI:12
April argument	*Frogpond* XXVII:1
spring sunshine	*Modern Haiku* 36:2
summer night	*Frogpond* XXVIII:2
smell of matches	*The Heron's Nest* VII:12
summer sunset	*Frogpond* XXIX:3
i can see us living	*Frogpond* XXIX:2
evening drizzle	unpublished
winter stars	*Frogpond* XXX:1
snowy evening	*Frogpond* XXX:1
winter beach	*Modern Haiku* 36:2
wintry spa	unpublished
winter beach	*Frogpond* XXVIII:3
nine months pregnant	*Frogpond* XXVI:3
spring planting	*Modern Haiku* 38:2

"spring morning" also appeared in the *Snapshots Haiku Calendar* 2006.

spring morning
the children's game
of being quiet

April argument
we can't suppress
our laughter

spring sunshine
the ladder i brought you
left behind

summer night
sounds of a concert
we could have attended

smell of matches
we recall the movies
that made us scared

summer sunset
the photographer
takes a step back

i can see us living
where we pass through—
summer travels

evening drizzle
not much to report
the second time i call

winter stars
my boy says he sees better
standing on the ground

snowy evening
no lights in the house
where there are problems

winter beach
the child decides
to let the stone be

wintry spa
mother looks at me
before accepting to dance

winter beach
a dog alternates
between its master and me

nine months pregnant
water drops
from icicles

spring planting
caught smiling at me
you won't say why

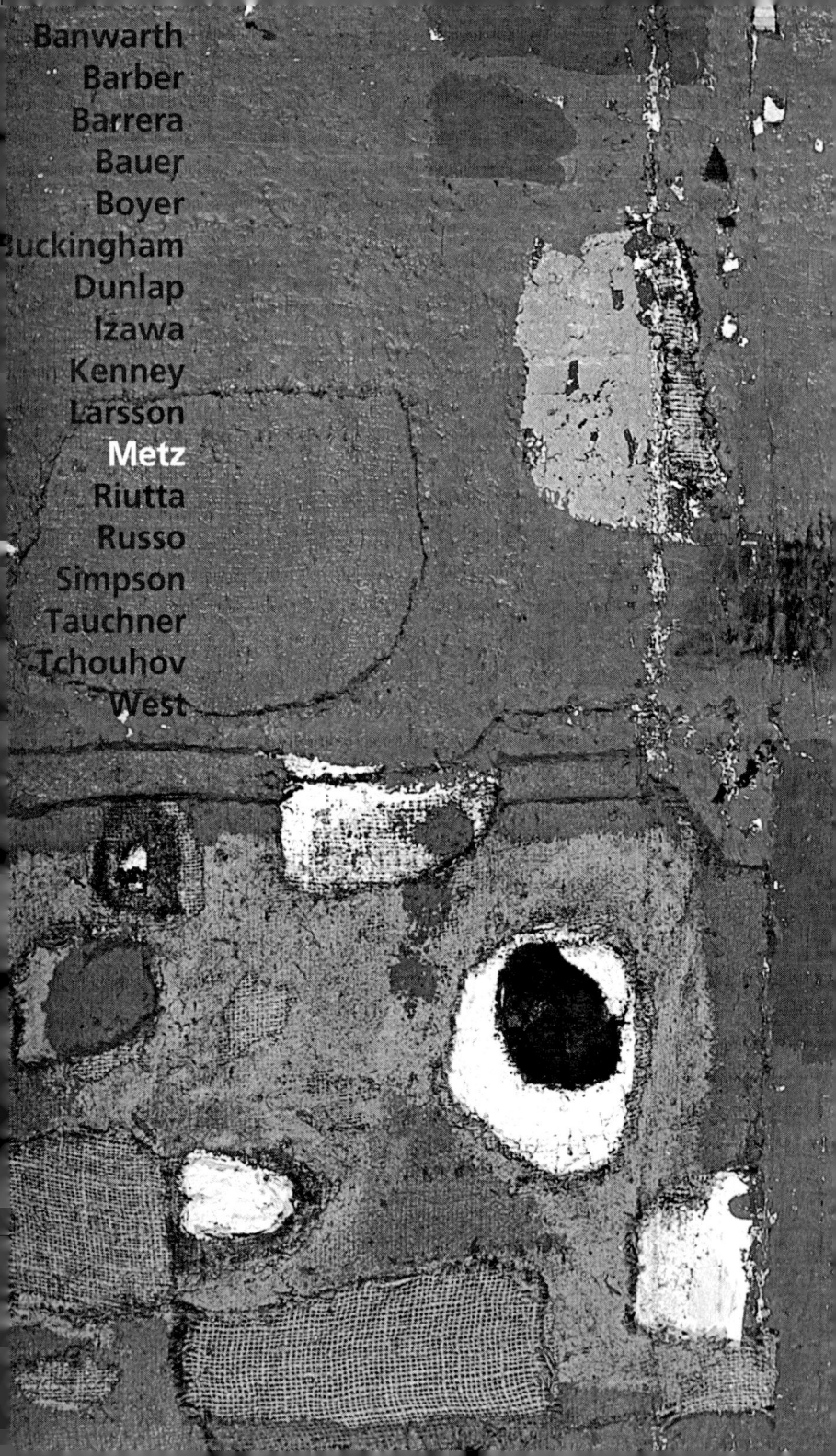

Scott Metz

Student

Born 28 November 1976
Allentown, Pennsylvania
Currently resides
Allentown, Pennsylvania

This poet has been largely in transition during the writing of most of these poems, and it shows—he is between countries, between jobs, between realities, and this betweenness colors the whole. There is a resistance here to rootlessness, an insistence on something central to personality and belief. When exoticism and novelty have worn off, we seek a return to identity that transcends place, hoping to keep what is valid of our new experience, but even more, hoping to be well-met and at home in the end.

Credits

New Year's Day	*Modern Haiku* 36:3
spring snow	*Hummingbird* XVI:3
darkness	*Acorn* 17
in spring rain	*NOON* 3
among the waves	*Frogpond* XXVII:1
more rain	*Modern Haiku* 37:3
reading the news	*Frogpond* XXIX:1
about to leave	*Frogpond* XXVII:1
after peeling	*Frogpond* XXIX:3
children outdoors	*Frogpond* XXVIII:3
autumn heat	*Acorn* 16
end of summer	*Modern Haiku* 37:1
autumn rain	*RAW NerVZ* X:4
first frost	*Acorn* 16
first spring bird	*Acorn* 16

New Year's Day—
the wreath has fallen
between the doors

spring snow
all day long
clinging to nothing

darkness gathering spring onions

in spring rain
a worker changing
the town's name

among the waves
in the Sea of Japan—
a woman's perfume

more rain the sisters slip into their mother tongue

reading the news
his fan slowly
becomes still

about to leave . . .
harvested rice fields
green a second time

after peeling my burnt skin new coolness

children outdoors
i finish the roof
of their Lego house

autumn heat reopening a scab

end of summer—
pressing her body against
the sea wall

autumn rain . . .
the parts i can eat
but don't want to

first frost . . .
the abandoned bicycle
further down the road

first spring bird . . .
she says it
before i do

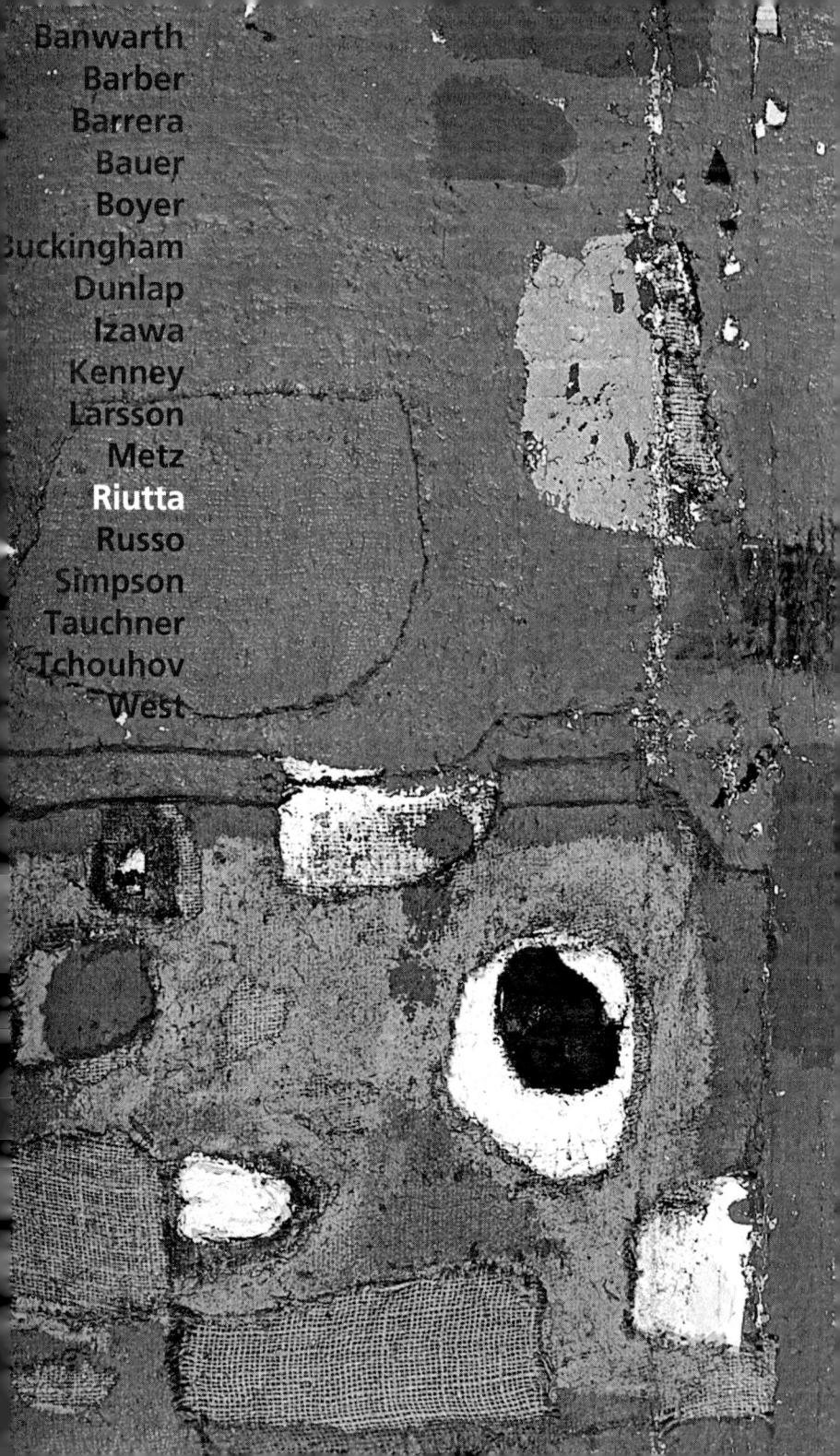

Andrew Riutta

Line Cook/Student

Born 30 June 1971
Keweenaw Peninsula, Michigan
Currently resides
Traverse City, Michigan

Riutta's work has a familiar feel to it—it could be the story of any family in a small town anywhere in the United States. The details, of course, will differ, and it is through the piling up of detail that the poet evokes for us his particular community. He trusts his material, leaving the stories inherent in these glimpses to tell themselves. The result is that the reader gets a feeling of the warp and weft of a social fabric, an ongoingness of which the poet is very comfortably a part.

(Photo by Lori Piggott)

Credits

apple blossoms	*Moonset* 2
spring breeze	unpublished
moonhaze	*f/k/a* website
unexpected death	unpublished
after the funeral	*Frogpond* XXX:2
in my coat pocket	unpublished
family ties	unpublished
cold drizzle	*White Lotus* 1
amongst crickets	unpublished
up and down	*Haiku Harvest* 5
a shut-off notice	*Shiki Kukai* January 2006
dark winter sky	*Shiki Kukai* January 2006
last call	unpublished
one day	*Reeds* 2006
apple wine	*Roadrunner* V:4

"a shut-off notice" also appeared in *big sky: The Red Moon Anthology 2006;* "apple wine" also appeared in *inside the mirror: The Red Moon Anthology 2005.*

apple blossoms
my grandfather snaps
his suspenders

spring breeze
on an old stump
I straighten bent nails

moonhaze
getting too old
for secrets

unexpected death
the steady hum
of an electric fence

after the funeral
the weight of potato salad
on a spork

in my coat pocket
through births and deaths
the same empty matchbook

family ties
the seal broken
on pickled beets

cold drizzle
onion skin clings
to a widow's hand

amongst crickets
I recite his eulogy
to myself

up and down
the teeter-totter
moonlight

a shut-off notice
flaps in the wind
midwinter

dark winter sky
the bright OPEN sign
of a liquor store

last call
the woman I doubt
doubts me as well

one day
becomes another
the sound of snow

apple wine
his story better
the second time

Dave Russo

Technical Writer

Born 9 November 1952
Salem, Virginia
Currently resides
Cary, North Carolina

Poetry, wrote Wordsworth, is "emotion recollected in tranquility." Haiku, for all its professions of residing in the here and now, exactly fits this schema, and no one better exemplifies this than Russo. These poems, though couched in the present tense, are pervaded by a quiet loneliness devoid of desperation emanating from their source in the poet's recollection. Throughout we find this poetic strategy, combined with a precision of language and a touch of *weltschmerz*, contributing to this unique voice.

(Photo by Lila Russo)

Credits

dirt road moon	*Simply Haiku* 4:4
roasting a rattlesnake	unpublished
walking alone	*Modern Haiku* 37:2
summer's end	*Modern Haiku* 29:3
too hot to sleep	*Frogpond* XXV:2
sun steams the rain	*Frogpond* XXII:2
first night in the dark	unpublished
sun in the bones	*Frogpond* XXV:2
It's late	*Modern Haiku* 27:3
last kiss	unpublished
galax leaves	unpublished
Father's Day	unpublished
prickly heat	unpublished
a neon violin	*Modern Haiku* 31:1
autumn afternoon	"Haiku Journey"

"summer's end", "too hot to sleep", "sun steams the rain", "sun in the bones" and "autumn afternoon" all appear in the computer game "Haiku Journey."

dirt road moon
frogs we gigged
heavy in the bag

roasting a rattlesnake we talk about girls

walking alone ghost water down a dry creek

summer's end
cicada buzz caught
　in the black cat's mouth

too hot to sleep . . .
from the fire truck's siren
a map of the streets

sun steams the rain
from the reservoir walls . . .
your laugh drifting by

first night in the dark together her parrot mumbling

    sun in the bones
     of a darting minnow
      my cell phone rings

It's late, the office
almost empty. Your bare feet
whisper by my door

last kiss the elevator waits for her body

galax leaves
shine on the next mountain;
missing her a little

Father's Day
empty snap hooks
clang the flag pole

prickly heat
looking for her grave
all over again

a neon violin
hums by the window
granddad's rented room

autumn afternoon
the teacher sits a while
by the window

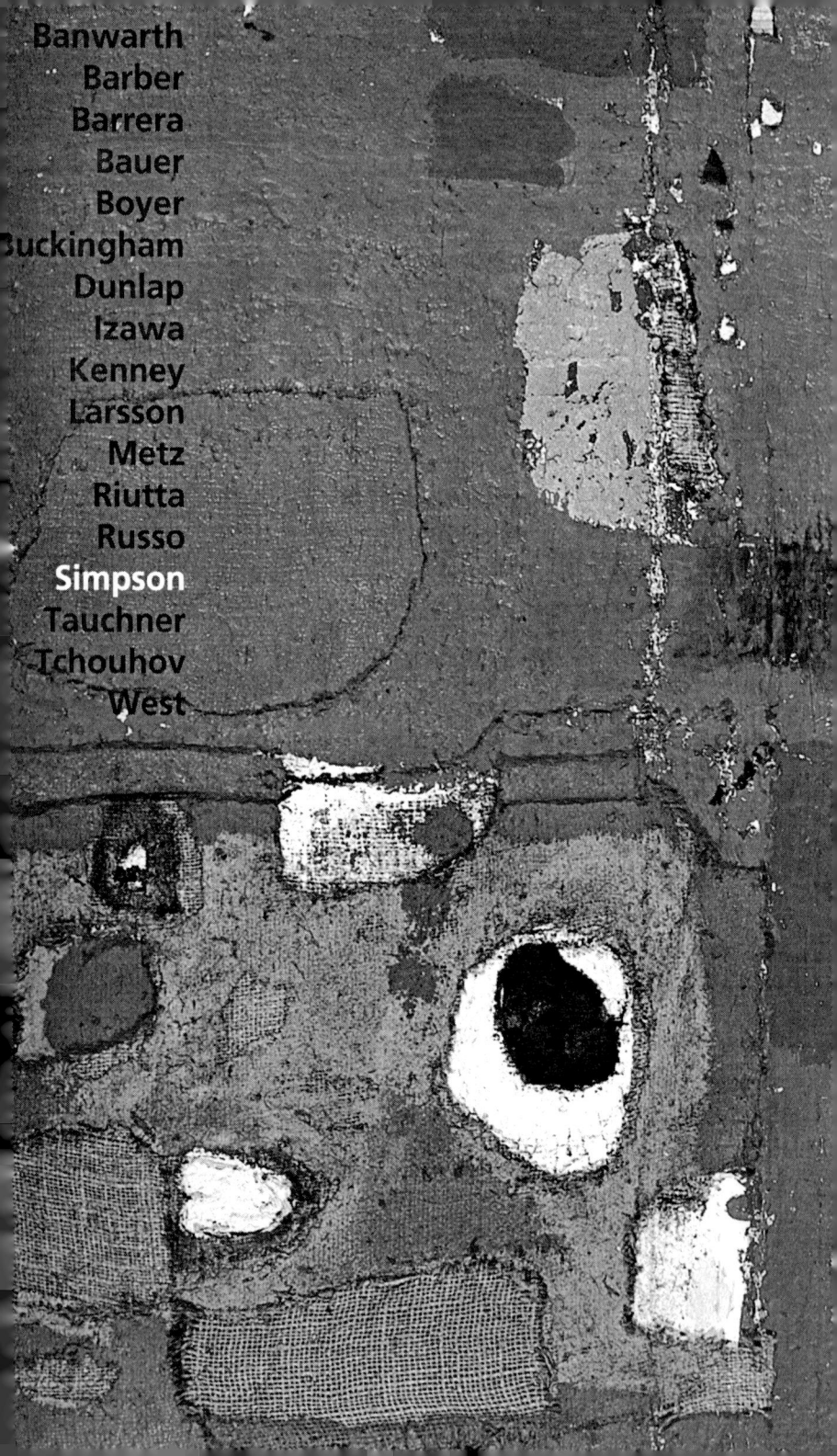

Sandra Simpson

Journalist/Mother/Poet

Born 15 August 1958
Ohakea, New Zealand
Currently resides
Tauranga, New Zealand

If we are to write not only for other poets, but for all, we must be willing to share the joys and travails that we all hold in common. Simpson attempts this larger goal, and her work registers the uncertainties of life and the hesitancies we feel before them. Her subject matter often tends toward the somatic if not the sensual. As a result these poems say "Here I am not," the only and ultimate testament to living any of us can make.

Credits

dry season	*The Heron's Nest* VII:1
tangi	*Frogpond* XXIV:1
waves break on the shore	*Kokako* 4
winter afternoon	*The Heron's Nest* VI:3
painting bamboo	*Simply Haiku* 3:1
cold morning	Vancouver Haiku Contest 2006
first butterflies	Suruga Baika Haiku Contest 2005
practising with chopsticks	*Lynx* XX:3
summer's end	*The Heron's Nest* III:7
on the sandbar	*Simply Haiku* 3:1
still damp	unpublished
summer storm	unpublished
picking raspberries	*Simply Haiku* 4:2
standing naked	*The Heron's Nest* VI:5
rain today	*The Heron's Nest* V:7

"waves break on the shore" won First Prize in the *Kokako* Haiku Contest 2006; "first butterflies" won an Honorable Mention in the Suruga Baika Literary Festival Haiku Contest 2005; "cold morning" was a Top 30 Poem in the Vancouver Cherry Blossom Festival Haiku Contest 2006.

dry season—
rock paintings
by a vanished people

tangi—
outside the wharenui
kids mixing shoes

tangi = traditional Maori funeral

waves break on the shore
your plane disappears
waves break on the shore

winter afternoon—
finding the needle
with my finger

painting bamboo—
trying to imagine
the wind

cold morning
amongst the blossoms
our pink fingers

first butterflies
catching the breeze
her new skirt

practising with chopsticks
she picks up
a new friend

summer's end
beachstore buckets on dusty shelves
anyoldhow

on the sandbar . . .
my footprints
going the other way

still damp
I wrap myself
in your towel

summer storm
the rolling white
of a horse's eye

picking raspberries
the sun
in my mouth

standing naked
in moonlight—
the taste of nashi

rain today—
her kimono
tied more loosely

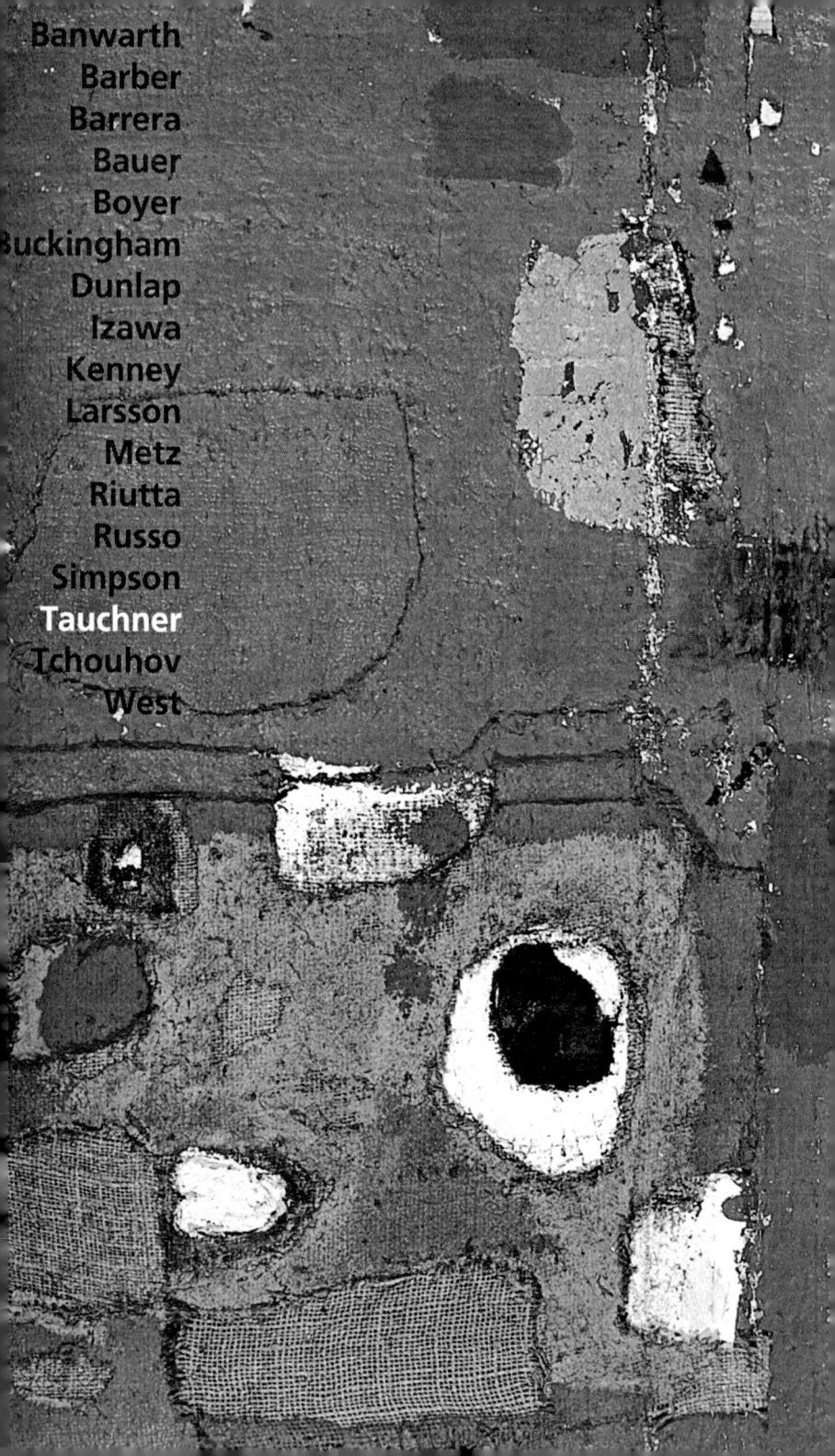

Dietmar Tauchner

Poet/Social Worker

Born 14 June 1972
Neunkirchen, Austria
Currently resides
Puchberg, Austria

Despite the veneer of culture we adopt, we humans are also animals, with animal drives and needs. Perhaps we are nearer to this truth when alone, and these poems of solitude, and the quest and longing for companionship, are closer to that animal existence than might always be comfortable. Interestingly, once the full extent of our inner nature is accepted, something more seems to become possible. All this the poet captures tellingly and with great economy.

Credits

spring longing	*The Heron's Nest* VII:4
nothing written	*South by Southeast* 13:1
swallows depart	*KO* Autumn/Winter 2005
departure day	*The Heron's Nest* V:8
gender god	*Roadrunner* VI:2
scented breeze	*Mainichi Daily News* June 3 2005
autumn rain	*KO* Autumn/Winter 2006
just before dawn	*Roadrunner* V:2
a new year	*KO* Autumn/Winter 2004
evening bells	*Modern Haiku* 35:3
first date	*Frogpond* XXVIII:3
frosty night	*Famous Reporter* 29
deep inside	*Roadrunner* VI:4
my key	*The Heron's Nest* VIII:2
spring morning	*Paper Wasp* 10:3

"nothing written" also appeared in *big sky: The Red Moon Anthology 2006*; "a new year" also appeared in *tug of the current: The Red Moon Anthology 2004*.

spring longing
following animal tracks
as far as I can

nothing written
on the trailhead sign
spring hike

swallows depart;
she comes back
to get her things

departure day
the car covered
with pollen

gender god gone deep in the woods

scented breeze
the inevitable glance at
the passing girl

autumn rain
the child touches my cheek
with a sponge

just before dawn—
the snowplow clears
my nightmare

a new year
the footprints
between graves

evening bells
a stranger's shadow
touches mine

first date
the sound of the motor
between us

frosty night
house by house the steam
of our talk

deep inside you no more war

my key
turns in the lock
lilac scent

spring morning
taking the road
towards the clouds

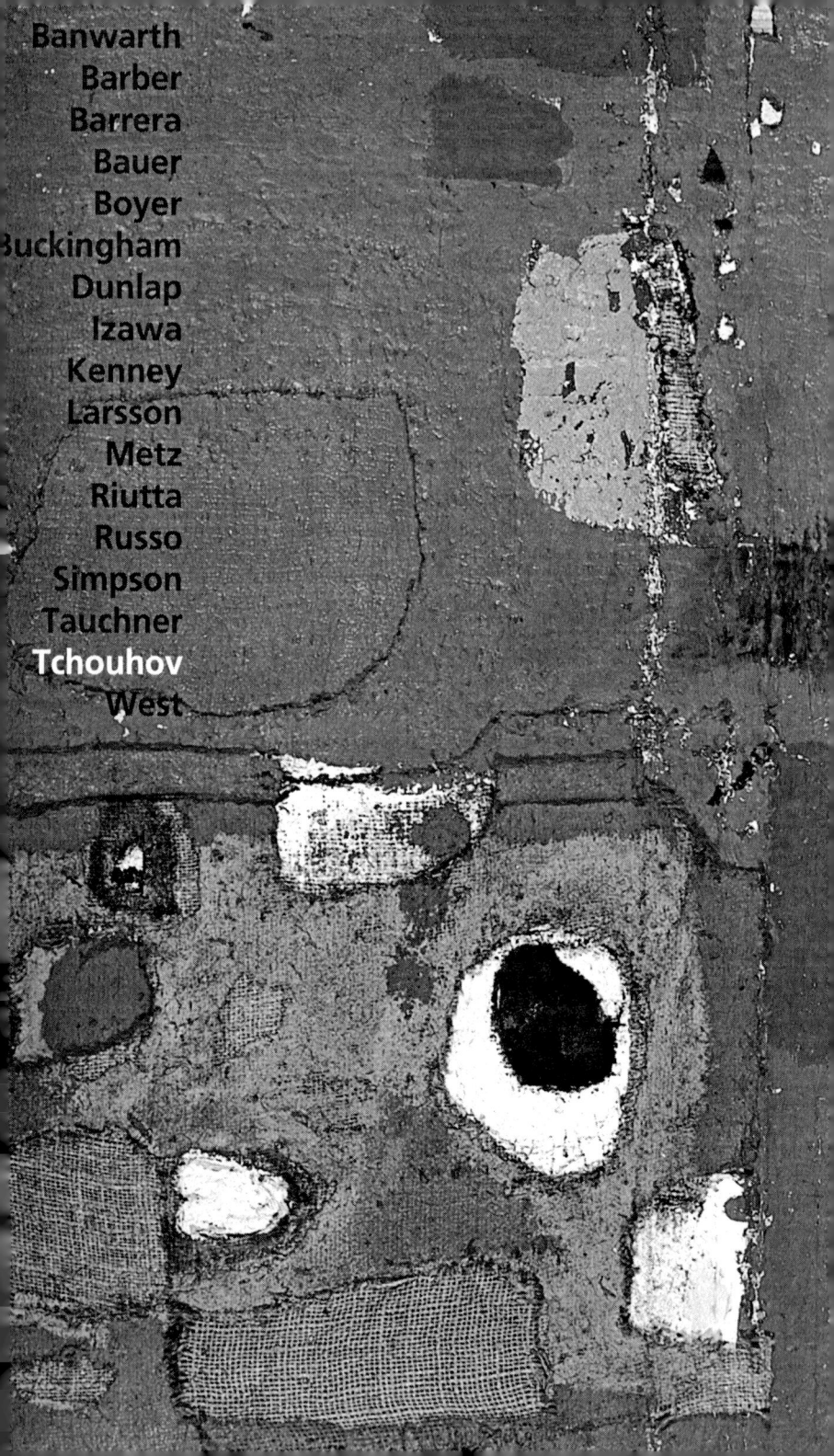

Petar Tchouhov

Poet/Musician/Translator

Born 23 June 1961
Sofia, Bulgaria
Currently resides
Sofia, Bulgaria

Of all the poets represented in this volume, Tchouhov is the most decidedly Old World in feeling and content. Throughout the work there is an axis of interchange between the animate and inanimate worlds, an almost medieval sensibility at work that sees other realities behind the surface that is apparent to all of us. The moment of their interaction is the moment of inspiration. The poet relates these moments to himself and to his God, and the result is an unexpected opening of the mundane to the numinous.

(Photo by Marica Kolcheva)

Credits

old calendar	*Shiki Kukai* January 2006
Sunday afternoon	*Clouds Peak* 2
candlelit church	*tiny words* 2March2007
the longest night	*Ginyu* 28
early thaw	*Shiki Kukai* February 2006
back from fishing	*Full Moon* 10
dog days	*Full Moon* 10
summer noon	*Presence* 26
healing mud	*Shiki Kukai* August 2006
after the earthquake	*World Haiku Review* 2006
in the grass	*Full Moon* 8
no man's land	*World Haiku Review* 2006
autumn wind	*Shiki Kukai* November 2005
the pinhead	unpublished
my father's birthday	*The Heron's Nest* VII:4

"old calendar" won 3rd Place in the January 2006 *Shiki Kukai*.

old calendar
my birthday marked
by my ex-wife

Sunday afternoon:
from the confessional—
singing

candlelit church
all the shadows
mine

the longest night
a raven steals the eyes
of a snowman

early thaw
her white bathrobe
missing

back from fishing—
a couple of pebbles
in my pocket

dog days
the weatherman's
new haircut

summer noon
in the shop window
naked mannequins

healing mud
we look as if God
has just made us

after the earthquake
a small crack
on the headstone

in the grass
near a swing—
a walking stick

no man's land
the air is cold
and clear

autumn wind
a stray dog unearths
a button

the pinhead—
almost part
of the butterfly

my father's birthday
I spill
a box of nails

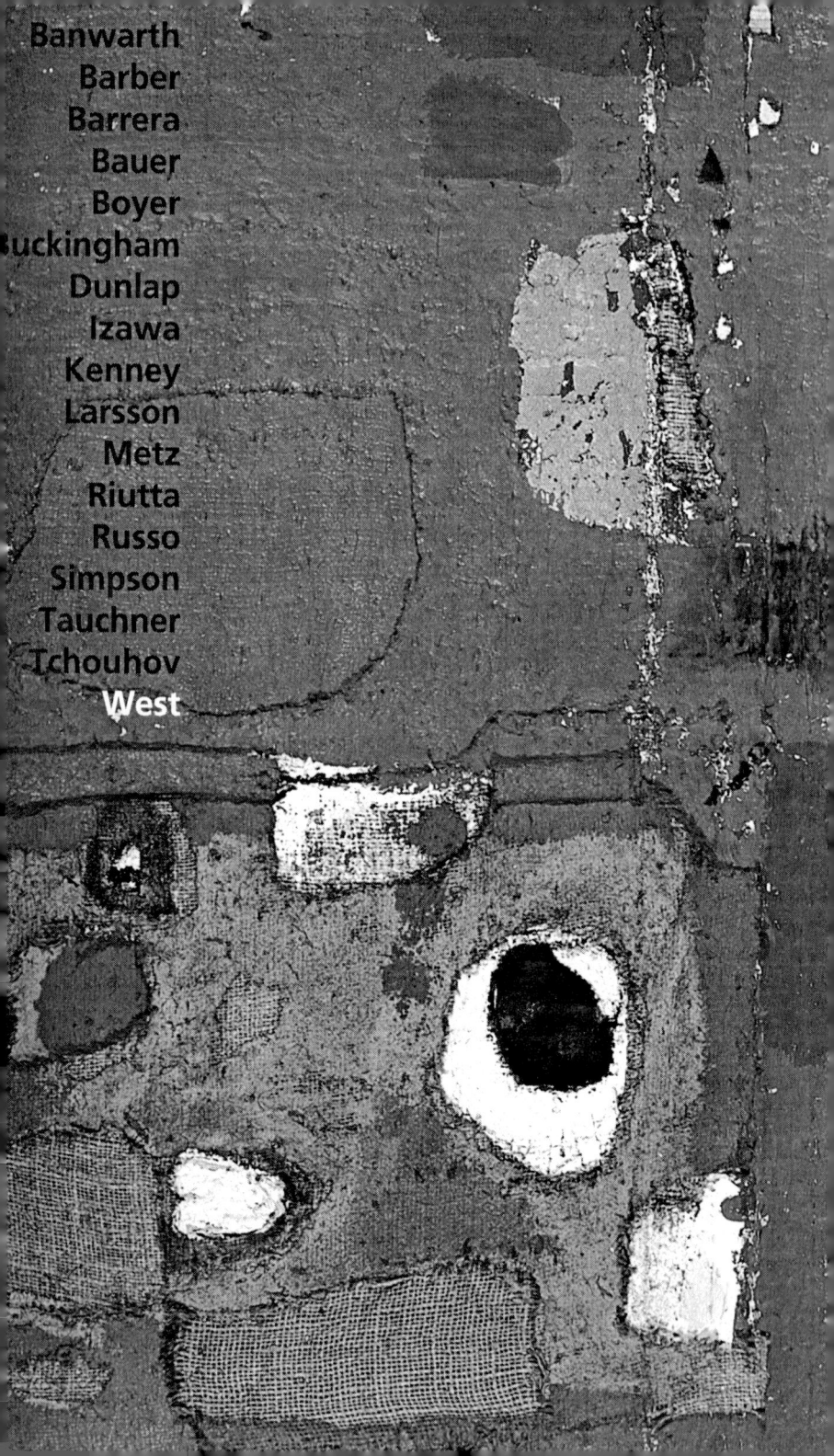

Banwarth
Barber
Barrera
Bauer
Boyer
Buckingham
Dunlap
Izawa
Kenney
Larsson
Metz
Riutta
Russo
Simpson
Tauchner
Tchouhov
West

Harriot West

Writer

Born 27 January 1945
Boston, Massachusetts
Currently resides
Eugene, Oregon

It is a wonderfully centering experience to be comfortable in one's skin, to recognize a correspondence between the inner and outer worlds of our existence. West seems to be just so comfortable as this, neither idle nor burdened, not goal-driven but capable of taking up the worthy cause. Her particular gift is finding ease without complacency and articulating it so the reader can find it too. Her subject is human activity, though in the old haiku tradition she finds a seasonal awareness that occasions her noticing.

Credits

the hiss of air	*The Heron's Nest* VIII:2
morning fog	unpublished
long day	*Frogpond* XXVI:3
autumn rain	*Modern Haiku* 38:2
joint custody	*Modern Haiku* 38:1
rainy afternoon	*White Lotus* 3
after the funeral	unpublished
memorial service	*Frogpond* XXX:1
winter stars	*White Lotus* 3
snowed in	*bottle rockets* 15
forsythia	*Frogpond* XXIX:3
dawn	unpublished
"Ode to Joy"	*Modern Haiku* 38:2
wicker chair	*Acorn* 14
summer afternoon	*Acorn* 15

"the hiss of air" won 2nd Editor's Choice for its issue as well as Special Mention in the 2006 *Heron's Nest* Readers' Choice Awards, and appeared in *big sky: The Red Moon Anthology 2006;* "summer afternoon" also appeared in *inside the mirror: The Red Moon Anthology 2005.*

the hiss of air
from a rubber raft
summer twilight

morning fog
the cheerful voice
of the weatherman

long day
trail dust swirling
down the drain

autumn rain
she reaches for
last year's knitting

joint custody
they each save him
the wishbone

rainy afternoon
untangling another strand
of colored lights

after the funeral
rolling socks
into pairs

memorial service
for a moment I wonder
what to wear

winter stars
the slightest shiver
in a hot bath

snowed in
another crossword puzzle
with no peeking

forsythia
a shaft of sunlight
in the birdhouse

dawn
a kestrel shakes off
rain

"Ode to Joy"
the piccolo player
sits up straighter

wicker chair
unraveling
summer's heat

summer afternoon
riding the streetcar out
and back

Sources Cited

Books

Byrd, John (Editor) *First Australian Haik Anthology* (Brisbane, Australia: Australian Haiku Society, 2000)

Childs, Cyril (Editor) *New Zealand Haiku Anthology* (Wellington, New Zealand: The New Zealand Poetry Society, 1993)

—— *New Zealand Haiku Anthology* (Wellington, New Zealand: The New Zealand Poetry Society, 1998)

Cobb, David, Editor *Between the Clouds* (Iron Press, United Kingdom 2003)

Gallagher, D. Claire (Editor) *Crinkled Sunshine: The Haiku Society of America Members' Anthology 2000* (Sunnyvale, CA: HSA, 2000)

Gorman, LeRoy, Editor *beyond spring rain* (Haiku Canada Member Anthology 2002)

Gorman, LeRoy, Editor *these silent rooms* (Haiku Canada Member Anthology 2003)

Kacian, Jim *et. al.* (editors) *a glimpse of red: The Red Moon Anthology of English-Language Haiku 2000* (Winchester VA: Red Moon Press, 2001)

—— *snow on the water: The Red Moon Anthology of English-Language Haiku 1998* (Winchester VA: Red Moon Press, 1999)

—— *the loose thread: The Red Moon Anthology of English-Language Haiku 2001* (Winchester VA: Red Moon Press, 2002)

—— *the thin curve: The Red Moon Anthology of English-Language Haiku 1999* (Winchester VA: Red Moon Press, 2000)

—— & Bruce Ross, Editors *stone frog: American Haibun & Haiga Volume 2* (Winchester VA: Red Moon Press 2001

karkow, kirsty *A Net of Sunlight* (Waldoboro, ME: Foothills Press, 2002)

Lanoue, David, Editor *The Haiku Society of America Members' Anthology 2003* (New Orleans, LA: HSA, 2003)

O'Connor, John, Editor *An Exchange of Gifts* (Christchurch, New Zealand: New Zealand Poetry Society , 2001)

Pollozzolo, John (Editor) *Raku Teapot: Haiku* (Alton Bay, NH: Raku Teapot Press, 2003)

Savina, Zoe, Editor *the leaves back on the tree: International Haiku Anthology* (Athens, Greece: Ekdosais 5+6, 2002)

Sheirer, John, Editor *Bridge Traffic* (Tiny Poems Press 1998)

Small White Teapot Group *listening to the rain: Anthology of Christchurch Haiku* (Christchurch, New Zealand: Small White Teapot Group, 2002)

Welch, Michael Dylan, Editor *Brocade of Leave* (Haiku North America 2003)

Journals, Magazines, Newspapers & Online Publications

Acorn, Blithe Spirit, bottle rockets, Cornell University Daily Haiku website, Frogpond, GEPPO, Haijinx, Haiku Canada Newsletter, Haiku Harvest, Haiku Headlines, Haiku Light, Haiku Presence, (The) Heron's Nest, Illinois Times, Mariposa, Mayfly, Midwest Poetry Review, Mie Times, Modern Haiku, paper wasp, pawEprints, Presence, RAW NerVZ, Snapshots, South by Southeast, still, Stylus, Solares Hill, Takahe, Wildwalk Haiku Kukai, winterspin, World Haiku Review.

Contests

Betty Drevniok Haiku Contest, Gerald Brady Senryu Contest, Harold G. Henderson Haiku Contest, Hawai'i Education Association Haiku Contest, Kusamakura International Haiku Contest, Mainichi Daily News Haiku Contest, New Zealand Poetry Society Haiku Contest, Novi Sad International Haiku Contest, PEN Women/Palomar Branch Haiku Contest, Suruga-Baika International Haiku Contest, Tallahassee Writers' Association Haiku Contest, Yellow Moon Seed Pearls Haiku Contest.